And The Sea Lay Down

Sermons And Worship Services For Lent And Easter

Elaine M. Ward

CSS Publishing Company, Inc., Lima, Ohio

AND THE SEA LAY DOWN

Library of Congress Cataloging-in-Publication Data

Ward, Elaine M.
    And the sea lay down : Lenten sermons and worship services for Lent and Easter/
Elaine M. Ward.
        p.   cm.
    Includes bibliographical references.
    ISBN 0-7880-1543-5 (pbk. : alk. paper)
    1. Lenten sermons. 2. Easter— Sermons. 3. Children's sermons. 4. Sermons, Ameri-
can. 5. Worship programs. I. Title.
BV4277.W37   2000
252'.62—dc21   99-052793
                                                                    CIP

This book is available in the following formats, listed by ISBN:
    0-7880-1543-5   Book
    0-7880-1544-3   Disk
    0-7880-1545-1   Sermon Prep

PRINTED IN U.S.A.

To Carl Jung, Annie Dillard,
James P. Carse, Mary Oliver,
and all the saints who write and have written,
helping "the sea lay down" for me.
With deep appreciation.

Table Of Contents

Introduction   7

Ash Wednesday   11
    A Time For Tears

First Sunday In Lent   19
    The Season Of Sacred Stories

Second Sunday In Lent   27
    Let It Go!

Third Sunday In Lent   35
    The Word Jesus Spoke

Fourth Sunday In Lent   41
    All-Surrounding Grace

Fifth Sunday In Lent   47
    "Unless A Grain Of Wheat ..."

Palm Sunday   55
    The Lord Has Need Of It

Maundy Thursday   63
    Jesus, The Servant

Good Friday   71
    Crumbs From The Cross

Easter Sunday   77
    Standing On The Shore

Lenten Poetry   83

Introduction

Sweet Jesus, talking
   his melancholy madness,
      stood up in the boat
         and the sea lay down,
silky and sorry.
   So everybody was saved
      that night.
         But you know how it is
when something
   different crosses
      the threshold — the uncles
      mutter together,
the women walk away,
   the young brother begins
      to sharpen his knife.
         Nobody knows what the soul is.
It comes and goes
   like the wind over the water —
      sometimes, for days,
         you don't think of it.
Maybe, after the sermon,
   after the multitude was fed,
      one or two of them felt
      the soul slip forth
like a tremor of pure sunlight,
   before exhaustion,
      that wants to swallow everything,
         gripped their bones and left them
miserable and sleepy,
   as they are now, forgetting
      how the wind tore at the sails
      before he rose and talked to it —

tender and luminous and demanding
   as he always was —
      a thousand times more frightening
      than the killer sea.[1]

The poem is based on Mark 4:35-41, a parable about the power of trust in God, for Jesus was grounded in the power of the Spirit. Storms catch us off balance, the violence of their power paralyzes us, the strength of their onslaught causes us to doubt and cry out, for there are risks in our passages through the sea, i.e. life. Crossing is not easy, but the journey is worthwhile. Like the disciples we fear, lack trust, have no faith. Jesus rebuked the storm "and the sea lay down."

I am overwhelmed by the number of books, sermons, stories, discussions, arguments about Jesus. For some Jesus is "sweet," for others he is "more frightening than the killer sea." As a preacher, teacher, parent, and pewperson I have heard the name of Jesus since childhood, learned and told his stories, and even experienced his presence in my faith imagination.

Once, tossed by an angry sea in a violent, traumatic windstorm in my own life, I dreamed I was drowning and cried, "Jesus, help me! Don't you care that I am perishing?" and the Voice returned, "I taught you to swim." Then in my great fear and need, Jesus "stood up" in my "boat," "and the sea lay down." I believe, as Jesus said, that he comes to those who have need, for that is when I am most aware of him in my life.

When I was a child, I walked to church. As an only child I walked alone, memorizing hymns and Bible stories, especially Jesus' parables. It began my love for poetry, the closest genre to parables, and my love for Jesus, the ultimate poetry of God.

These Lenten sermons (meditations, worship services) concern Jesus' passion, death, and resurrection. I have borrowed my title, *And The Sea Lay Down*, from Mary Oliver's poem, "Maybe," above.

The disciples awoke their master out of their fear of the wind and the waves, the storm of the sea. That is when, as I said, I "shout at" Jesus, knowing he knows suffering, doubt, and fear. I once heard

8

of a woman who was terrified of the water her husband loved. With her Bible group she agonized over her helplessness and they told her this story over and over. She learned it and said it aloud until at last she heard Jesus speak the words to her, "Peace! Be still!" And the sea lay down. The wind ceased and there was a dead calm. One day she even invited her group to go sailing with her husband and her. It was a day of celebration and thanksgiving! What healed the woman? Was it the story she heard repeated over and over? Was it because of the people who supported her during her fear? Was it because she finally believed for herself, trusted God? Or was it God, Creator of wind and waves, death and new life who healed the woman? Jesus is the center that holds, bridges, and acts when we ask.

Jesus stood up in the boat and talked to the wind and the sea lay down. Because he brought peace to an angry sea, an angry crowd, a confused people, today we remember how "tender and luminous and demanding he always was."

The biblical stories, especially the stories of Jesus' passion, death, and resurrection, form and feed and transform our faith. The soul needs feeding. As the poet says,

Nobody knows what the soul is.
It comes and goes
   like the wind over the water —
  sometimes, for days,
     you don't think of it.

Poetry's function is not to define nor explain but to create images we can see and stories we can enter. Thus, believing in the power of parables, poetry, and the power of Christ through prayer, these meditations are offered, and with the disciples and the sailors I pray, "We are so small and our boat is so small and the sea is so great, Lord, help us all!"

And the sea lay down.

---

1. Mary Oliver, *New and Selected Poems* (Boston: Beacon Press, 1992), pp. 97-98.

A Time For Tears

Call to Worship
"O Lord, open my lips, and my mouth will declare your praise" (Psalm 51:15). Come, let us worship the Lord with our praise.

Processional Hymn
"Come, Thou Almighty King" (words: Anonymous; music: Felice de Giardini, 1769).

Children's Time
The child was late. Her mother was worried. When the child finally returned home, the mother anxiously asked, "What happened? What kept you so long?" "I stopped to help my friend who was crying over her broken doll," the child replied. "Oh, did you help her fix her doll?" asked her mother. "No, I stopped to help her cry."

Talk About
Tears are a way of letting feelings out. Do some things make you sad? What makes you cry? What helps when we are crying? Does it help someone to cry with them?[1]

Prayer of Confession
"Have mercy on us, O God, according to your steadfast love; according to your abundant mercy, blot out our trangressions" (Psalm 51:1). Forgive us our trespasses as we forgive those who trespass against us. "Create in us a clean heart, O God, and put a new and right spirit within us" (v. 10).

Words of Assurance
"The grace of the Lord Jesus Christ, the love of God, and the communion of the Holy Spirit be with all of you" (2 Corinthians 13:13). Amen.

Psalter Reading Psalm 51:1-17

Old Testament Joel 2:1-2, 12-17

Epistle Lesson 2 Corinthians 5:20b—6:10

New Testament Matthew 6:1-6, 16-21

Sermon
When Jesus came to Golgotha they hanged him on a tree.
They drove great nails through hands and feet and made a Calvary.
They crowned him with a crown of thorns, red were his wounds
    and deep,
For those were crude and cruel days and human flesh was cheap.

When Jesus came to Birmingham they simply passed him by.
They never hurt a hair of him, they only let him die;
For men had grown more tender, and they would not give him
    pain;
They only just passed down the street, and left him in the rain.

Still Jesus cried, forgive them for they know not what they do,
And still it rained a wintry rain that drenched him through and
    through.
The crowds went home and left the streets without a soul to see
And Jesus crouched against the wall, and cried for Calvary.
(Author unknown)

    This is Ash Wednesday, a day of tears and ashes. Jesus cried for Calvary. The child stopped to cry with her friends. We cried in confession, "Have mercy on us, O God, according to your steadfast love."

    Lent is a time for tears, a season for crying. Facing the prospect of a torturous, agonizing death on a cross, Jesus cried, "My heart is breaking. And what should I say, 'Father, save me from this hour'?" But Jesus rejected human weakness. "No, it is for this reason that I have come to this hour."

It was midnight and after three hours of waiting in the emergency waiting room, she placed her jacket on the arm of the chair and tried to sleep. Sleep, however, was replaced by hearing again the frantic telephone call she had received earlier that evening. It was a cry for help from a son suffering from deep depression and now physical pain. One more blow struck at his frail body and even weaker mind. She felt her helplessness while waiting. All she could do was pray, let go, and experience the ashes and the tears. "Let this cup pass from me, from my son. No more, Lord. Enough." And finally, exhausted, "Thy will be done."

The poets know this kind of pain and loneliness.

No time ago
or else a life
walking in the dark
    I met Christ
    jesus, my heart
    flopped over
    and lay still
while he passed (as
close as i'm to you
    yes closer
made of nothing
except loneliness[2]

The poet e e cummings wrote of his experience of meeting Christ one night. Ash Wednesday is a night for tears and loneliness and ashes.

Asher Lev, born with the gift of drawing, drew everywhere, all of the time, while he slept and ate, walked the streets or studied. But Asher Lev was a Hasidic Jew for whom idols, such as paintings and sculpture, were forbidden. They also distracted Asher from studying the Torah, the word of God for the Jews. Against his father's will, however, Asher continued his pursuit to express his truth through paint. His gift led him to study scenes of the crucifixion in the museum of his beloved Brooklyn and finally in Florence, Italy, where he saw the *Pieta*, Jesus dead, lying in the lap of

13

his mother. He saw in her face the face of his mother. It was his mother who had kept the gift alive during the dead years, while trapped between her husband's aversion to, even hatred of, Asher's gift, and her son's love for painting. After studying the *Pieta*, Asher felt his mother's torment as she waited endlessly by the living room window for her husband and her son to return home, fearing that someone she loved would be brought to her dead.

As an adult Asher moved to Paris, but for months he could not paint, and he walked the winter streets, feeling their coldness. He simply stood and stared at the empty canvas on his easel. At last, however, it came. It had been coming for a long time, as Asher knew, trying to choke it as he had, hoping it would die. Yet there was no other way to do it. With charcoal he drew the long vertical of the center strip of wood in the living room window of his Brooklyn home and the slanted horizontal of the bottom of the venetian blind. Behind those two lines Asher drew his mother, her right hand resting on the right side of the window, the left hand against the frame over her head, her eyes directly behind the vertical line, burning through it. He drew the verticals and horizontals of the telephone poles and painted it in dark, smoky colors. It was a good painting but it was incomplete. The telephone poles were only distant reminders of the brutal reality of a crucifix. It did not fully speak of the anguish and torment he wanted to express. The voice within Asher spoke of fraud, of the difference between integrity and deceit in a created work.

For days he felt the incompleteness of the painting. Then at last, on a canvas the same size, he sketched the window and blinds and this time he drew his mother on top of the window, her arms outstretched, along the horizon of the blinds, her wrists tied to it with its cord, her legs tied at the ankles to the vertical of the inner frame with another piece of the cord. He arched her body and twisted her head. He drew his father standing to her right, dressed to travel, carrying an attache case, her son at her left in paint-spattered clothes, holding a palette and spearlike brush. Her son painted in her mouth, the twisting curve of the head, the arching of the body, the clenching of her small fists, the taut downward pointing of her thin legs, as the tearing anguish he felt in her. Asher Lev, an observant Jew, worked on the crucifixion because there was no symbolic mold in his own religious tradition into which he could pour his feelings of ultimate anguish and torment. Asher Lev, another Jew, felt the agony of his own crucifixion through the cross. This was the final break with his family and community, for rivers of Jewish blood had been shed over this scene. His own grandfather had been killed by a drunken Christian on the eve of Easter.

In choosing this work, he pained his father. Because he was a sensitive artist painting out of his own suffering and the suffering he saw about him, his paintings caused more pain in those who saw them. Pondering, as he walked the streets for hours, thinking about the meaning of his gifts as an artist, he talked to the Master of the Universe. "Will I live this way all the rest of my life?" "Yes," came the whisper from the branches of the trees. "Now journey with me, my Asher. Paint the anguish of all the world. Let people see the pain. But create your own molds and your own play of forms for the pain. We must give a balance to the universe." Asher Lev chose to create with God, to begin again out of the ashes.[3]

Lent is the season of crying and carrying our cross, for after the tears we take up our cross, seeing it now as God's transformation of our human cruelty into the symbol of God's suffering love.

For all things there is a season,
A time for crying and a time to rejoice,
A time for ashes and a time for palms,
A time for suffering and a time to dance,
A time to confess and a time to give thanks,
A time to wait and a time to worship, love, and celebrate.
A time for tears and a time for treasure
For where your treasure and your tears are,
Your heart will be also.

So give balance to the universe, Asher, Alice, Arthur, begin again out of the ashes to new life in Christ. Amen.

Hymn
"My Faith Looks Up To Thee" (words: Ray Palmer, 1830; music: Lowell Mason, 1831).

Invitation to Come Forward
I invite you in the name of the church of Jesus Christ to receive the ashes of penitence placed on the forehead as a sign of repentance and forgiveness, remembering our dependence upon God.

Distribution of Ashes

Affirmation of Faith
I believe in God, Creator of life and love and laughter. And Jesus Christ, who knew and showed us how to live that love and laughter even through our tears. And the Holy Spirit who enables us to cry for the suffering in our world and to change what we can change from tears to laughter. In Christ's name. Amen.

Prayers of the People, the Pastor, and the Lord's Prayer

Pastoral Prayer
Most gracious, loving Lord, with these ashes we are reminded of death, ashes to ashes, dust to dust. As rain refreshes the earth and new life is born, take our tears and in your mercy turn them into the triumph of your cross and resurrection, new life in Christ. As you led your people of old, lead us through the wilderness of this Lenten season transforming our wilderness into a new world filled with your glory, in your name. Amen.

Offering

Doxolgy

Hymn of Commitment
"O Love That Wilt Not Let Me Go" (words: George Matheson, 1882; music: Albert Lister Peace, 1884).

Benediction

Go now in the name of God who collects our tears, and Jesus the Christ who weeps for and with us, and the Holy Spirit who enables us to begin again. Amen.

---

1. Elaine M. Ward, *Love in a Lunchbox: Poems and Parables for Children's Worship* (Nashville, Tennessee: Abingdon Press, 1996), p. 96. Used with permission.

2. e e cummings, *Haipe,* ed. George James Firmage (Liveright Publishing Corp., 1979).

3. Chaim Potok, *My Name is Asher Lev* (New York: Fawcett Crest, 1972).

The Season Of Sacred Stories

Call to Worship
"You are my Beloved; with you I am well pleased." Come, let us worship the divine Parent.

Hymn of Procession
"Holy, Holy, Holy! Lord God Almighty" (words: Reginald Heber, 1826; music: John B. Dykes, 1861).

Children's Time
"It's ugly!" the ducks quacked together. "Is it really my duck?" asked the mother duck. One duck flew up and bit the ugly duckling in the neck. The chickens stood and stared, as the poor ugly duckling was bitten, pushed, and jeered at. It did not know what to do, where to stand or walk, and was so sad because it was ugly and different from the others.

Day after day the poor duckling was picked at; its sisters and brothers made fun of it, the girl who fed them kicked it with her foot, and even its mother wished it were far away.

And so one day the ugly duckling flew over the fence and came out into a great field, where the wild ducks lived. Sad and lonely, it lay in the tall grasses for two whole days. At last one of the wild geese said, "You are so ugly, I like you. Come with us."

But before the duckling could decide, the sky was filled with loud snapping sounds and two of the geese fell into the swamp, dead. The ugly duckling put his head under his wing, lying quite still, as the shots rattled through the reeds.

When the storm of shells was over, the storm of nature began. Rain and thunder and lightning. The duckling raced across the field until he came to a small, miserable hut. Frightened and exhausted, he slipped through the crack in the door into the house of the woman who lived there with her hen and her cat, and he was allowed to remain.

19

Then autumn came. The leaves turned yellow and brown. The wind tossed them about, the air was cold, and the clouds hung heavy with hail and snow. Winter was very cold. The ice froze. One morning a farmer found the duckling frozen fast in the ice. He broke the ice with his shoe and rescued the duckling.

But at last the day came when the sun began to shine again and the larks to sing, for it was spring. The duckling flapped his wings and beat the air and flew more strongly than ever before, finding himself in a great garden, where from the thicket he could see three glorious white swans, swimming lightly in the water.

"But what is this?" he asked, seeing his image in the clear water. He was no longer a clumsy dark gray bird, ugly to look at, but a beautiful, graceful swan! Swimming through the water, he thought, "It matters not if one is born in a duck yard, if one has lain in a swan's egg." The old swans stroked him with their beaks and bowed their heads before him. Once an ugly duckling, he hid his head, under his wing, because he was so happy.[1]

Prayer of Confession
Loving Parent, who calls us to live as a family in this world, we confess we have ignored your command. We have built barriers between families and neighbors, communities and nations. Though we say we are one in Christ, we look with suspicion and fear on those who are different from us. Forgive us our doubts, the hurts we have done, and have mercy on us all. Create a new spirit within us that we may walk with you in your way. In the name of your son, Christ Jesus. Amen.

Words of Assurance
The loving father saw his prodigal son from a far distance and ran to him, throwing his arms around him and celebrating his return. Jesus said God was that loving father. Amen.

Psalter Reading Psalm 25:1-10

Old Testament Genesis 9:8-17

Epistle Lesson   1 Peter 3:18-22

New Testament   Mark 1:9-15

Sermon

Garrison Keillor has said that if you are shy and from the Midwest and Lutheran, it is always Lent. Lent comes from the Anglo-Saxon word *lecten* meaning "spring." Its liturgical color is purple, signifying both humility and royalty. In the early church Lent was a time to prepare for baptism, which took place on Easter Eve. Lent is the forty day period between Ash Wednesday and Easter (excluding the six Sundays), a symbolic reminder of the forty days of the Exodus of God's people in the desert and the forty days of Jesus in the wilderness before his ministry. Today Lent is known as a time of deepened discipleship, a period of preparation and penitence, the season of the soul and the sacred story.

Lent is the time for remembering the stories of Jesus' happy entrance into Jerusalem on Palm Sunday, of his Last Supper with his friends, the horror of his crucifixion, and the glory of his resurrection.

Mark tells the story of "the good news of Jesus Christ, the Son of God." His intent was to tell us both what the good news is and who Jesus, that "good news," is — the Son of God. Mark writes, "Just as he (Jesus) was coming up out of the water, he saw the heavens torn apart and a voice came from heaven." Throwing aside all majesty and transcendence God shouted out, "You are my Beloved; with you I am well pleased." Jesus saw and heard and in that hearing was ordained for his mission by the Spirit of God, the dove, the sign of life on earth. The voice spoke an intimate word to Jesus who had come to John ready to take his place among sinners and instead he received unconditional acceptance and assurance from God.

"And the Spirit descended like a dove on him." And all the people rushed into the river with their needs and desires, their labels and illusions, seeking to crown him king, but because the dove was nesting there, there was no need for a golden crown. The words robed him in his mission and he rose from the waters to bring God's essence into a waiting world.

Mark does not tell us, but our faith imagination can hear the angels applauding, the small ones cheering him on, as the dove cooed and the waters around and above him bubbled with joy.

In Mark there is no birth narrative for Jesus. We might say, when Jesus entered the River Jordan, God "jumped out" at him with the words, "You are my Son, the Beloved; with you I am well pleased." A college student told her friend the way her mother had explained her birth: "According to my mother, the way I was born is that she went to the A & P and when she came home, I jumped out from behind the kitchen door and surprised her."[2]

I believe God speaks, reveals, "jumps out" in the way we are open to that encounter, that relationship with God. To some through nature. Others through scripture, Christ, prayer, music, dance, or art. Some through stories, for our very life is an unfolding story of our encounter with God.

The "Jordan" is the symbol of our willingness to listen, to find our mission, our work. To step into the Jordan is to risk rather than to search for ways to remain safe and dry on the shore, for while we are wandering in grief and longing, God jumps out and says, "You are my beloved son, daughter. No longer do you need to live out the story of the abused, the abandoned, the anxious one. You are accepted! I am delighted in you!"

Once, during a trying time, I awoke from sleep and in that half consciousness heard the Voice, "You will know what to do when you get there." They were my "beloved daughter" words and I have lived by them ever since.

God jumps out at us through the events of our lives. The goal of worship is to allow the story of God's love to be grasped by all of our senses, to see our lives resonate with that story and to tell our own.

They had climbed the stairs wearily, heavy with the truth they were delivering. Their knock had been loud and impatient, angry as the news they carried. The four-year-old child had looked up from her play to watch her mother cross the room. She had listened to the murmurs of the sad voices and then her mother's cry. Although she did not hear it that night, the message the police had pronounced was of her father's death. He had been killed immediately as the car he was driving catapulted into the passing train, for the car's brakes had failed.

Just as quickly she had been hurtled into God's arms, her adopted Father, although she did not know it then or as she matured. How could she know when her church taught her that God was an angry judge? She rejected that "father," for there was always a flickering flame of remembrance of her daddy's love.

As she grew she searched for her absent Parent, for do we not all project upon God the image of our human parents? And having been taught to think rather than feel, she was unaware that the absent parents, both the human and the divine, were with her all along.

Then one day God "jumped out" at her in the form of a woman, a healer of wounded healers. Attending a retreat for wounded healers, the healer heard her story and said, "I think you have repressed your anger over your wounds. Let it out. God can take it. God loves you. Are you willing to invite Jesus into your faith imagination?"

Wounded, she agreed, and to her amazement became the four-year-old child in her imagination, remembering the healer's words, "Tell Jesus how it feels to lose a parent as a small child." She shared her story, her feelings of loss and confusion, and when it was over, dried her eyes and smiled. "Now what do I do?" she asked the wise woman.

"Take time with Jesus in your imagination. Talk with him. Give your anger to him." The woman did not mean tomorrow, nor next week, nor sometime in the future. Her words meant now.

The wounded one wandered to the tiny prayer chapel the wise woman had built in her back yard. She sat in silence and waited for Jesus to come into her imagination. It was a long wait. At last she spoke, no longer the four-year-old, but an angry woman. "If you will not come, then I will leave!" And Jesus replied, "Come sit on my lap." The four-year-old refused. Jesus smiled, and this time Jesus waited.

Slowly, cautiously, she came and crawled up into his lap. "All children need daddies," he said, putting his arms around her. "I am sorry your daddy was killed. I cannot bring him back now, but I have a gift for you. Reach into my pocket." Tentatively, shyly, she put her hand into the pocket of his robe and found the gifts of imagination and trust and clasped them to her heart, no longer alone. Nor would she ever be alone again, for no one could take the gifts Jesus had given her. She had not earned them. They were gifts and, in her imagination, suddenly her father was with her. At last she knew she was loved.

The season of Lent is the season of sacred stories. Telling stories during Lent gives substance to our hopes and fears, our faith and doubt. They are our inner selves speaking the language of the imagination, the way we reveal who we are and what we love and value. They grow out of our lives and nourish our lives, and some reveal God in our lives, for that is where we find God.

With Christ in our faith imagination stories can change our lives, for God says to us all, "You are my beloved. In you I am well pleased." In that story and those words may we live and move and have our being. Amen.

Hymn
"Lord, To You My Soul Is Lifted" (based on Psalm 25, words: Stanley Wiersman, 1980; music: Louis Bourgeois 1551; harm. Howard Slenk, 1985).[3]

Prayers of the People, the Pastor, and The Lord's Prayer

Pastoral Prayer
God of the reformers, renewers, resisters, give us strength and direction and keep our feet from falling and straying. Send us hope for our despair, purpose for our path, and obedience to our inheritance. Open our ears to the message of Lent.

Affirmation of Faith
I believe in God, our divine Parent and in Jesus Christ who showed us what it means to be a child of God, and the Holy Spirit who enables us to learn and live in that love. Amen.

Offering

Doxology

Hymn
"Our Parent, By Whose Name" (words: F. Bland Tucker, 1939;
music: John David Edwards, ca. 1838).

Benediction
Go now in the name of the heavenly Parent, and Christ, God's
beloved Son, and the Holy Spirit who calls us into that presence in
Christ's name. Amen.

---

1. Hans Christian Andersen, *The Complete Hans Christian Anderson Fairy Tales*
   (New York: Avenel Books, 1984).
2. James P. Carse, "Exploring Your Personal Myth," *Sacred Stories* (San Francisco: Harper, 1993) p. 223.
3. # 178, *The Presbyterian Hymnal* (Louisville, Kentucky: Westminster/John Knox
   Press, 1990).

Let It Go!

Call to Worship
Jesus said, "Come to me, all you that are weary and are carrying heavy burdens, and I will give you rest" (Matthew 11:28).

Processional Hymn
"God Of Grace And God Of Glory" (words: Harry Emerson Fosdick, 1930; music: John Hughes, 1907).

Children's Time
There is an old story that tells of three trees growing on a hillside, dreaming of what they wanted to be. The first said, "I want to be a treasure box and hold the greatest treasure in the world." The second said, "I want to be a strong sailing ship and carry the most powerful king in the world." The third said, "I want to grow tall and point to God who gives beautiful treasures and mighty seas."

Their dreams grew as the days passed until one day men came with axes and took away the three trees. The first tree became a box to hold hay for the animals to eat. The second tree became a boat to hold fishermen and their smelly fish. The third tree was sawed and planed and left a plank, and many years passed.

One quiet night the cows mooed softly as the young mother placed her sleeping baby in the box that held the hay. "It will be his manger," she said. Then the small box knew it held the greatest treasure in the world, God's gift of love in Jesus.

More years passed and one stormy night the waves rose high as the wind tossed the small fishing boat to and fro. Jesus' friends were frightened, but he stood up and said to the waves, "Peace, be still!" And the sea lay down. And the boat knew he was carrying the most powerful king.

Then more years and one dark night a crowd of angry men nailed Jesus to the cross that was the third tree. But on Sunday morning the sun shone and Jesus lived again and the tree knew that whenever people saw the cross, they would remember God, for the three trees' dreams had come true.[1]

Prayer of Confession
Dear Lord, we are "rich in things and poor in soul." Our fears and doubts have too long bound us. Free our hearts to work and praise. Grant us wisdom and courage for the living of these days. Amen.

Silent Prayer

Words of Assurance
Jesus said, "I know that and I love you." Amen.

Psalter Reading   Psalm 22:23-31

Old Testament   Genesis 17:1-7, 15-16

Epistle Lesson   Romans 4:13-25

New Testament   Mark 8:31-38

Sermon
Long ago there was an ancient bell that was famous for its beautiful tone. It had been commissioned by the king. The king's advisors had told him that making a huge temple bell would secure the nation from foreign invasion. The specialist who cast the bell had produced several failures until he concluded that the only way to produce a great bell was to sacrifice a young maiden. Soldiers were sent to find and fetch such a young girl. Coming upon a poor mother in a farm village with her small daughter, they took the child away, while she cried out piteously: "Emille, Emille!" — "Mother, O Mother!"

When the molten lead and iron were prepared, the little girl was thrown into the fire. At last the bell maker succeeded. The bell, called the Emille Bell, made a sound more beautiful than any other. When it rang, most people praised the art and the artist that had created such a beautiful sound. But whenever the mother whose

28

child had been sacrificed heard it, her heart broke anew. Her neighbors, who knew of her sacrifice and pain, could not hear the beautiful tone without pain either. Only those who understand the sacrifice can feel the pain. Others just enjoy the sound.[2]

Pain and suffering are with us. Turn on the television, read the newspaper, listen to your neighbor or a member of your family. Suffering is part of authentic living and the greatest courage is the courage of suffering. When we face a fate that cannot be changed, an incurable disease, a broken relationship, the suffering of our beloved, what matters above all is the attitude we take toward our suffering. Yet how often we feel sorry for ourself or the suffering one. They do not want our pity, however, but our companionship.

Perhaps it matters less what we expect from life than what life expects from us. Our answer consists of action and responsibility.

Jesus taught them that the Son of Man must undergo great suffering and be rejected — and be killed — and rise again. Peter rebuked him, but Jesus to Peter, "Get behind me, Satan! For you are setting your mind not on divine things but on human things." He called the crowd and said to them, "If any want to become my followers, let them deny themselves, and take up their cross and follow me."

Recently, I ran away like a child escaping the "no's" of life. Caught between a 93-year-old mother who wants to die and can't and a 42-year-old son who wants to live and can't, for two weeks I escaped. I pretended they could "do their work" without me.

Have you ever wanted to do that or done that, be it only a long walk to escape pressing problems, to gain a more positive perspective, to let nature heal? The last day of my escape to another's son's home, he read to me from Viktor Frankl's *Man's Search for Meaning*. I said, "I have to buy this book!" Searching his library, he found another copy and presented it to me.

Have you ever had that experience? A "coincidence," a "chance happening" of the right book or person appearing at the right moment? As a lover of stories I believe it is one of the ways God communicates.

Perhaps you are wondering, however, what was so important about the book. It is Frankl's account of his years in the concentration camps of the Holocaust, of his suffering and his survival. Given his experience, his words ring with authority: "If there be a meaning in life at all, then there must be a meaning in suffering. Without suffering and death human life cannot be complete."[3]

"If any of you wish to follow me, you must take up your cross," Jesus said.

All of us carry worries and burdens, desires and disappointments. All of us experience suffering and sometimes even ask, "Why doesn't God relieve pain and suffering? Where is God's power? Can God be all-powerful and all-loving? Where was God during Emille's sacrifice? Christ's suffering?" But what if divine power is not like human power?

Satan knew human power — turning stones into bread, jumping off of the temple (or the cross), ruling the earth. God's power however, is in the sheathing of the sword, comforting the chicks, coming out of the temple to climb up onto the cross.

God's power certainly isn't used to do for me what I can do for myself, nor does it seem to answer my need for the healing of the suffering of ones whom I love. We live without the assurance of the power of God but in the promise of the presence of God.

"If you want to be my follower," Jesus said, "you must deny yourself." There are many things we have to "let go." One of them is the demand for answers and for God's power as we wish it. I think the poet said it correctly: "To live in this world/you must be able/to do three things:/ to love what is mortal;/ to hold it/against your bones knowing/your own life depends on it;/and, when the time comes to let it go, to let it go."[4]

Remember the final scenes of *Indiana Jones and the Last Crusade*? The woman could not let go of her greed to obtain the Holy Grail and in that desire lost her life. Indiana too wanted to capture it and his father told him to let go. "I can almost reach it," Indiana replied, as his father gently reminded him, "Indiana, let it go."

There is new life in letting go. Unaware of the harm of holding on to bad relationships, life-denying perspectives, and self-defeating projections, we are like the bear that wandered into camp, seized the boiling pot, and, screaming with pain, was unwilling to let it go.

Sometimes we pray for God's power in our lives to ease or remove the suffering, while still clutching the habits and actions that cause them.

But these are abstract words. Hear then this story: A woman once wore a sword in her breast, but because she did not want to burden others with her wound and suffering, she covered it with her cloak. One day she met a woman, groaning and moaning and groping in the dark. "What is the matter?" she asked. The other told her that she was blind and in need of a staff, and the woman who could see looked around but could find no staff. At last she took the only thing she had, the sword in her heart, and gave it to the blind woman who, using it, exclaimed, "This is a good staff!" For the first time the woman understood the meaning of the sword and her suffering.

In the last twenty years there has been a doubling in the suicide rate. A sense of hopelessness, meaninglessness, boredom, or the desire for intense excitement has led to an increased use of drugs and alcohol. Affluency and lack of acceptance of "delayed gratification" are other reasons for suicide.

When you have lost your job, your spouse, the usefulness of your body, when you see suffering and injustice all about, what does it mean that "all things work together for good for those who love God"? Is Paul promising too much? Perhaps before the wounds of the world the best things would be to keep silent. Yet Job didn't. Paul didn't either. He interpreted his suffering through the cross of Christ and interpreted the cross through his suffering.

Jesus told us to take up our cross and follow him. The world breaks everyone but some become strong at the broken places. Do you remember the film *Regarding Henry*, in which a highly successful lawyer became a helpless vegetable of a man in a moment? We too are vulnerable, for it is a real world out there. I live downtown and get up in the dark, in the middle of the night for some of you. Hardly a night passes without the sirens of police, ambulance, and fire truck breaking the deep silence. It keeps prayer life active, as a friend reminds me, whenever I avoid the bad news of newspaper or television, "Then how do you know for whom to pray?" Because I do not know who suffers in those accidents outside my window, my prayer is "Thy will be done," for I believe that God wants the best for us, wants harmony and well-being for all of us. I believe in the love God pours into us through the Holy Spirit, for God does not send suffering but is with us in the suffering, in God's promise "I will be with you."

"My friend isn't back from the battlefield, sir. I request permission to go out and get him." "Permission denied," the officer said. "I will not have you risk your life for a man who is probably dead." The soldier went all the same and in an hour returned mortally wounded, carrying the corpse of his friend. The officer was furious. "I told you he was dead. Now I have lost both of you. Tell me, was it worth going out there to bring back a corpse?" The dying man replied, "Yes, it was, sir. When I got to him, he was still alive. And he said to me, 'Jack, I was sure you would come.' "[5]

Jesus came. And when he came he said, "Take up your cross and follow me." Amen.

Hymn
"In The Cross Of Christ I Glory" (words: John Bowring, 1825; music: Ithamar Conkey, 1849).

Pastoral Prayer
Lord, you know our pains and our prayers. In Christ's name give us the courage to carry our cross. Praise be to Thee. Amen.

Offertory

Doxology

Hymn of Consecration
"Take My Life And Let It Be (words: Frances R. Havergal, 1873; music: Louis J. F. Herold, 1839).

Benediction
Go now in the name of God who is with us in our suffering, and Jesus the Christ who shows us how to suffer, and the Holy Spirit who enables us to hope and endure in our suffering. Amen.

1. If you wish to show children pictures as you tell the story, see Angela Elwell Hunt's illustrated *The Tale of Three Trees* (Oxford: Lion Publishing, 1989). (adapted)

2. John S. Pobee and Barbel von Wartenberg-Potter, *New Eyes for Reading* (Geneva: World Council of Churches, 1986), pp. 19-20.

3. Viktor E. Frankl, *Man's Search for Meaning* (New York: Pocket Book, 1939), p. 106.

4. Mary Oliver, *New and Selected Poems* (Boston: Beacon Press, 1992), p. 178.

5. Anthony de Mello, *Taking Flight* (New York: Doubleday, 1980), p. 147.

The Word Jesus Spoke

Call to Worship
"Thy word is a lamp unto my feet" (Psalm 119:105). Come, let us see, walk, and worship in the word of the Lord.

Processional Hymn
"O Word Of God Incarnate" (words: William Walsham How, 1867; Neuvermehrtes Meiningisches Gesangbuch, 1693; adapt. Felix Mendelssohn, 1847).

Special Music
"Thy Word Is A Lamp Unto My Feet" (words: Amy Grant, 1984; music: Michael W. Smith, 1984; arr. by Keith Phillips).

Children's Time
Winnie the Pooh woke up one morning hungry, but his honey pot was empty so he decided to go for a walk and soon came to Rabbit's hole, which meant company, which meant honey for Pooh's hunger. Rabbit invited Pooh in and served him honey and concentrated milk and bread. When the honey was gone, Pooh said he had better be gone too, and Rabbit said he was going out, as well.

So Pooh climbed out the front door. He put his nose out and then his head and then he pulled ... and pulled ... and pulled, but he was stuck. "Help!" Pooh cried. Rabbit pushed and pushed and said, "I think you ate too much." "No, your door is too small," Pooh replied. "Go get Christopher Robin." So Rabbit went out the back door.

When Christopher Robin returned, he looked at Pooh's head sticking out of the rabbit hole, sat down, and thought, "Well, Pooh, I think you are here until you get thin." Pooh began to sigh and then he found he couldn't because he was so tightly stuck; and a tear rolled down his eye, as he said, "Please, Christopher Robin, will you tell me Sustaining Stories, such as would help and comfort a Wedged Bear in Great Tightness?"[1]

Talk Together
What does "Great Tightness" mean? What is your favorite story? Who reads to you? What words of Jesus help you when you are sad or need comforting?

Prayer of Confession
Sometimes we forget our need for "sustaining stories" that help us in great tightness. Forgive our forgetting your words during the dry deserts of our lives and the dark forests where we feel helpless and hopeless. Remind us of those who need our presence and our stories. Amen.

Words of Assurance
Jesus reminds us: "My words and my presence will never pass away."

Psalter Reading   Psalm 19

Old Testament   Exodus 20:1-17

Epistle Lesson   1 Corinthians 1:18-25

New Testament   John 2:13-22

Sermon
When the Israelites heard the first word of the Law in the Ten Commandments, so the old rabbinical story goes, they swooned. Their souls left them. So the word returned to God and cried out, "O Sovereign of the Universe, you live eternally and your Law lives eternally. But you have sent me to the dead. They are all dead!" Thereupon God had mercy and made his word more palatable.[2] God told a story.

Our sacred story for today said that they believed the scripture and the word that Jesus had spoken. Long before, Jesus had said to

36

his disciples, "Heaven and earth will pass away, but my words will never pass away."

At the end of the conflict stories in Mark Jesus left the Temple for the last time. Sitting on the Mount of Olives, looking down at the Temple, he told his friends of the new temple, which would bring in God's time and the new heaven and earth. "Listen!" Mark told his congregation. Listen to the shaking of the foundations. Nothing is permanent. Everything is change. Heaven and earth will pass away. Mark was writing his words to a community that had finally revolted against the Roman rule and had failed, to a community trying to make sense out of a chaotic world. The temple where God resided and ruled had been destroyed. The revolt was a defeat. All that remained were a few at Masada awaiting their death. To this community Jesus' words created a new world, connecting life with God beyond the Temple, in the world here and now, and they asked, and continue to ask, for a response. "Whose words will you follow?"

There is a war of myths. The Roman government has its myth. The revolutionaries have their myth. The temple priests have theirs. It is true, as well, today. Madison Avenue has its myth: "Buy! Buy!" Big business has its myth: "Money is power!" The government of the United States has its myth: "My country right or wrong." Because a myth is the story by which we live, out of which we act, it is a sustaining story. Jesus' words tell us of a loving, generous Parent who forgives, preparing a banquet for our return. They tell of an enemy who helped heal another by pulling him out of the ditch, of a Shepherd who hunted for the little, lonely, and lost, a Creator who sends rain on the just and the unjust, and counts each hair of our head.

Jesus' words invited his hearers to hear and see in a radically new way, for sacred stories have that power, the power to change a person and a people at their very roots. And Jesus was in his word, inviting us to dwell in his word. Jesus was the Word. Words are symbols. They mean more than they say. They are rich in meaning. The poet wrote, "I am evading a definition. If it is defined, it will be fixed and it must not be fixed ... To fix it is to put an end to it" (Wallace Stevens).

Jesus said, "I am the way, the truth, the light, the door, the vine, the shepherd," as a storyteller who spoke in symbols. I believe in their reality. Most poets, preachers, and "profess-ers" of faith do. "A poet's words are of things that do not exist without the words." In the speaking and writing of words, they are given life. They become what they express, as God sent out God's word to do what it was meant to do.

Words are our stumbling, inarticulate, sometimes amazing way of expressing what we feel and think about invisible, eternal realities, the world of the spirit. Yet, just as we are one in body and soul, so the worlds of spirit and of flesh are intertwined.

Words provide a way by which to see. They have the possibility of making our meaning. The poet W. H. Auden once said that poets write because they like "hanging around words."

Sometimes
the writer
of words,
restless and
divinely discontent,
Jacob-like
struggles with
these angelic creatures
until they name.
Sometimes
the writer stands aside
waiting,
listening
for what they
have to say.
And sometimes
patiently,
gently,
the writer leads them
as a flock
beside still waters.

The disciples believed because of the words of Jesus and of scripture. Faith is believing in God. The poet Robert Frost was once asked what made him think he could write a poem. He simply "believed in it." He said that the most creative thing of a child, a man, or a woman was to believe in a thing. Because the disciples believed, they carried Jesus' words into the world, and they have never passed away.

Jesus' words touched the deep places of his hearers' heart. His hands touched their bodies, their eyes and ears, as he healed and blessed them, and with his touch and his words said, "I am here."

God has a "word" for each of us: "Agnes, feed my sheep. Philip, love one another. Bradley, follow me." And when we "eat" and enflesh God's words, they come alive among and within us. "Heaven and earth will pass away, but my words will never pass away." They will be a part of you as long as you exist — which is forever. Praise be to God! Amen and Amen!

Hymn of Response
"Wonderful Words Of Life" (words and music: Philip P. Bliss, 1874).

Prayers of the People, the Pastor, and The Lord's Prayer

Pastoral Prayer
Let us pray in the words of the preacher poet, George Herbert:

"Lord, how can man preach thy eternal word?
He is a brittle crazie glasse:
Yet in thy temple thou does him afford
    This glorious and transcendent place,
    To be a window through thy grace."[3]

Through thy Word and words ignite our inner resources, the Spirit within, so that we may hear and see the heart. Some days everything goes wrong, sometimes for a week, a month, a year. It seems as if all of our friends have unsolvable problems, that whatever we do fails, and we feel helpless and hopeless and unloved, so that we become bitter, hopeless, and in despair. Lord, give us hope so that out of that hope we accept your love and your word that gives meaning to our lives. Amen.

Offering

Doxology

Hymn of Commitment
"Thy Word Is A Lamp Unto My Feet" (words: Amy Grant, 1984; music: Michael W. Smith, 1984; arr. by Keith Phillips).

Benediction
Go now in the name of God who creates the Word, and Jesus the Christ who is the Word, and the Holy Spirit, who enables us to hear Jesus' words that never pass away.

----

1. A. A. Milne, *Winnie The Pooh* (New York: Dutton, 1926).

2. Rosemary Haughton, *Tales from Eternity* (New York: Seabury, 1973).

3. George Herbert, "The Windows," *The Country Parson, The Temple* (New York: Paulist Press, 1981), p. 103.

Fourth Sunday In Lent

All-Surrounding Grace

Call to Worship

Processional Hymn
"O God, Our Help In Ages Past" (words: Isaac Watts, 1719; music: William Croft, 1708; harm. by W. H. Monk, 1861).

Children's Time
The little island said, "I am part of the big world," and the cat replied, "No, you're not. Water is all around you and cuts you off from the land." "Ask any fish," said the island. The kitten caught a fish and asked, "How is an island a part of the land?" "Come with me," said the fish, "down into the dark secret places of the sea and I will show you." "I can't swim," said the cat. "Show me another way." The fish replied, "Then you must take it on faith what I tell you." "What's that?" said the cat — "faith?" The fish replied, "To believe what I tell you about what you don't know."[1]
   (Holding a Bible read John 3:16.)

Prayer of Confession
Dear Lord, we confess that our doubt limits and blocks our prayers that create possibility. We lose heart. We fear moving ahead. We lack courage, patience, and persistence for pursuing our dreams and expressing our faith that all will be well. Help us grow in hope to sing our song of faith from an overflowing heart. Amen.

Words of Assurance
God, our Maker, gives us songs in the night for the night. Amen.

Psalter Reading   Psalm 107:1-3, 17-22

Epistle Lesson   Ephesians 2:1-10

41

Sermon

>   As swimmers dare
>   to lie face to sky
>   and water bears them,
>   as hawks rest upon air
>   and air sustains them,
> so would I learn to attain
>   freefall, and float
> into Creator Spirit's deep embrace,
>   knowing no effort earns
> that all surrounding grace.
>   (Denise Levertov, *Oblique Prayer*)

God so loved the world ... that love, that unconditional love, is the foundation for our faith. John wrote, "God so loved the world that he gave his only Son, so that everyone who believes in him may not perish but may have eternal life." And at the end of his good news, he wrote, "These (stories) are written that you may believe that Jesus is the Christ, the Son of God, and that by believing you may have life in his name" (John 20:31).

We have those stories. It is all a matter of believing them. C. S. Lewis wrote such a story about Christ as the lion Aslan in the world of Narnia and when Lucy, human, stepped through the wardrobe, she was in another world. When she returned to share her good news with her two brothers and sister, they would not believe. Worrying over Lucy, they went to the professor with whom they were staying during the war and complained that when they looked through the wardrobe, there was nothing there. The children said, "If it was real why doesn't everyone find this country every time they go to the wardrobe? If things are real, they're there all the time. They don't change." The professor thought for a moment. Then he said out loud, as if he were still thinking to himself, "If there is a door in this house that leads to some other world ... if she had got into another world ..." "Sir," said Peter, "do you really mean that there could be other worlds — all over the place, just

42

round the corner, on some mountaintop, just like that?" The professor nodded his head. "Nothing is more possible," he said, wondering, "what do they teach these children these days?"[2]

Faith is trust in God, the willingness to believe until we can know. Faith acts and creates its own truth. If a train was about to be robbed and you believed that the rest of the passengers would back you up, out of that belief you could prevent the robbery. There are times when a fact cannot happen unless faith in the fact helps create the fact. If truth is dependent on our action, then faith based on possibility is indispensable.

I read of a dream a man had about his friend after the friend had died. He and his wife were staying overnight with the widow. In the dream he told his friend how much he missed him and then asked, "Are you really there?" "Of course," his friend replied, plucking a strand of blue wool out of his jersey and tossing it to the dreamer. The feel of the wool was so real the dreamer awoke from the dream. The next morning at breakfast he told the dream. His wife replied that she had seen a strand on the carpet as she was getting dressed that had not been there the night before. The dreamer, wide awake, rushed upstairs to see for himself and — there it was (Frederick Buechner).

What do your dreams tell you? John said that stories (perhaps dreams) were written so that we might believe.

When my sons were young and I read to them, it was *The Chronicles of Narnia* and *Wrinkle in Time* that enriched our sense of believing. In the latter, Meg, the heroine, asked her mother, a scientist, "Do you think things always have an explanation?" "Yes, I believe that they do. But I think that with our human limitations, we're not always able to understand the explanations. But you see, Meg, just because we don't understand doesn't mean that the explanation doesn't exist. I don't understand it any more than you do, but one thing I've learned is that you don't have to understand things for them to be." When Meg still did not understand, Mrs. Whatsit said, "Explanations are not easy when they are about things for which your civilization still has no words."[3]

Faith is believing beyound proof about "things" for which our civilization has no words. The dreamer of the dream suggested

43

that the strand of blue wool on the carpet, just a piece of wool, might be a sign.

"Give us a sign," we cry. Something from the "beyond" that is extraordinary to tell us that we are not alone, that we are surrounded by grace.

A thread of blue wool from a dead friend's sweater is too good to be true. To trust that we are surrounded by grace shatters our sense of meaninglessness. We can "float into Creator Spirit's deep embrace."

Faith is dynamic, changing, growing, decreasing, but doubt is not necessarily disbelief. Doubt can be re-visioning. Jacob, Job, and Jeremiah remind us that doubt can be the impetus to deeper trust, for faith is not proof, faith is beyond belief, trust that brings believing into being.

The dreamer thought that the blue wool could have been nothing more than a coincidence, but he believed, finding that thread that had not been there before the dream.

We have the sacred stories of scripture, of the desert fathers, of the Hasidic holy men. The rabbi saw a man in the marketplace so intent upon his business he never looked up. He asked him, "What are you doing?" The man answered hurriedly, "I have no time to talk to you now." The rabbi, however, refused to be snubbed and repeated his question, "What are you doing?" This time the merchant impatiently cried, "Don't delay me. I have to attend to my business." But the rabbi insisted. "Everything you are so worried about is in the hands of God and all that is in yours is to trust and love God."

The disciples in the boat in the storm were worried and Jesus said to them, "Why are you afraid? Have you no faith?"

The author of the book of Hebrews wrote that faith is the assurance of things hoped for, the conviction of things not seen (Hebrews 11:1). Charlie Chaplin mixed his comedy with tenderness. In the film *City Lights*, Chaplin is a tramp whom a rich man, intoxicated, rewards financially, but when he sobers up, he charges Charlie with the theft of his money. Charlie, meanwhile, has given the money to a blind girl for eye surgery and is caught and imprisoned. After serving his prison sentence, the tramp returns to the world and passes the flower shop of the formerly blind girl. She scorns him, only to discover the unkempt and forlorn tramp is her benefactor. Using her sense of blindness — touch — she feels his face and speaks the word, "You!"

During Lent we are introduced to that "You" in our lives. "God so loved the world he gave his only Son ..."

When Carl Jung visited Taos Pueblo in 1924 he spoke with one of the inhabitants, questioning him on his opinion of his neighbor, the white man. The Native American replied that his people believed that the white man was "mad." "Why?" Jung asked. "They say they think with their heads." Jung agreed that this was so and asked him how he thought. "We think here," he replied, pointing to his heart.

Faith, trusting in God and God's all-surrounding grace, is thinking with the heart, believing.

When the night was darkest and hope the faintest, in the fullness of time, God sent the gift of hope into the world, Jesus the Christ. So I would conclude with the words, the faith affirmation, of Puddleglum, the Marshwiggle in Lewis' *The Silver Chair*: When the White Witch had convinced the children that there was only darkness, and hope the faintest, Puddleglum replied: "Suppose we have only dreamed, or made up all those things — tree and grass and sun and moon and stars and Aslan himself. Suppose we have. Then all I can say is that, in that case, the made-up things seem a good deal more important than the real ones ... I'm on Aslan's side even if there isn't any Aslan to lead it. I'm going to live as like a Narnian as I can even if there isn't any Narnia."[4]

"These (stories) are written that you may believe that Jesus is the Christ, the Son of God, and that by believing you may have life in his name ... For God so loved the world that he gave his only Son ..." Amen.

Hymn of Response
"Of The Father's Love Begotten" (words: Aurelius Clemens Prudentius, 1851; music: eleventh century *Sanctus* trope; arr. by C. Winfred Douglas, 1940).

Prayers of the People, the Pastor, and The Lord's Prayer

Pastoral Prayer
Living Lord, we come all dressed up to worship, while what you ask is faith. Forgive us our lack of trust, of believing beyond belief. Not just for today here in the sanctuary but wearing our faith into the world this week, all week. Clothe us in your all-surrounding grace that we may freefall and float into your deep embrace. Create in us a clean heart and renew a faithful spirit within us. Amen.

Affirmation of Faith
I believe in God and in God's promise of all-surrounding grace, and in Jesus Christ who lived and died and lived again in that grace, and in the Holy Spirit who bears, sustains, and embraces us with that grace. Amen.

Offering

Doxology

Hymn of Commitment
"I Sing A Song Of The Saints Of God," (words: Lesbia Scott, 1929; music: John H. Hopkins, Jr., 1940).

Benediction
Go now into the world in the name of God whose grace surrounds us, and Jesus Christ who taught us to believe what we do not know, and the the Holy Spirit who enables us to risk believing into being. Amen.

---

1. Golden, MacDonald, *The Little Island* (New York: Scholastic, 1946).

2. C. S. Lewis, *The Lion, The Witch, And The Wardrobe* (New York: Macmillan, 1950).

3. Madeleine L'Engle (New York: Dell Publishing, 1962).

4. C. S. Lewis, *The Silver Chair* (New York: Macmillian, 1953), p. 159.

"Unless A Grain Of Wheat ..."

Call to Worship
Jesus said, "I, when I am lifted up from the earth, will draw all people to myself." Come, let us worship God who lifts us up.

Processional Hymn
"The God Of Abraham Praise" (words: Daniel ben Judah, 1404; music: Hebrew melody).

Children's Time
Once upon a time there was an old man and his wife who lived at the edge of a small mountain village in the snow country of Japan. One winter morning the old man set out for the village with a bundle of firewood to sell.

As he trudged through the falling snow he heard a pitiful cry, "Koh, koh." Turning from the path to look, he came upon a great white crane frantically trying to free herself from a trap. The old man had compassion for the magnificent bird and released the cruel spring of the trap. At once the crane flew up, joyfully calling, "Koh, koh," and disappeared into the snowy sky.

With a lighter step the old man went on through the snow, and when he returned once more to his humble home, he told his wife about rescuing the crane. "That was a good deed," she said. As she spoke, there was a tapping on the door. Opening the door, she saw a beautiful young girl standing in the swirling snow. "I have lost my way. May I share the warmth of your fire tonight?" she said. "My name is Tsuru-san." "Come in, poor child, before you freeze in the bitter cold," cried the old wife. Together they shared a simple supper of hot porridge, and then they gave her their bed with its warm quilts, while they slept the night huddled on a pile of straw.

In the morning the old man and the old woman were surprised to see a fire already burning on the hearth, the water urn filled with fresh water, the floors swept, and all the rooms clean and tidy. Tsuru-san was busily stirring a pot over the fire. "Good morning," she said, bowing to the old couple. "The porridge is cooked and ready." They were delighted and because Tsuru-san had no parents, it was decided she would remain as a daughter.

The children of the neighborhood found the girl a delight, as well, and the house rang with happy laughter. The hearts of the old man and the old woman were filled with joy and the early days of winter passed happily, but soon there was no money, therefore, no food. Tsuru-san said, "I wish to help. I will weave cloth for you to sell in the village." The cloth was as beautiful as Tsuru-san and sold quickly.

Tsuru-san continued to weave with only one request — not to be watched while she worked. But one day Curiosity caused the old woman to peek. There sitting at the loom was the white crane, pulling feathers from her body, weaving them into cloth. But now the Promise was broken. Her eyes filled with tears. "I can no longer stay with you." With a great whish of her wings, she flew up into the sky and the crane maiden was gone forever.

Talk Together
What did the crane maiden give? Why? What can you and I give? Jesus said, "Whoever loses his life for my sake will find it." And then he said, "Follow me."

Prayer of Confession
Loving God, forgive us our refusal to grow, to let go, to change, and create in us raw vulnerability, open receptiveness, and deep sensitivity through the cross that invites us to participate in our suffering and darkness. Help us let go of clinging to things so that you may become God in us. Amen.

Words of Assurance
God is God of Darkness and Silence as well as Light and Word. God is Both/And, Lord of History and of Creation. "Go your way, your trust has saved you." Amen.

Psalter Reading	Psalm 51:1-12
Old Testament	Jeremiah 31:31-34
Epistle Lesson	Hebrews 5:5-10
New Testament	John 12:20-33

Sermon

Moon had a message for man and woman and called Insect to come and carry the message to earth. The message of Moon was, "As I die and in dying, live, so you in dying will live also." Insect took the message of Moon to earth and on the way met Hare. "Where are you going?" asked Hare. "I have a message from Moon to man and woman. Moon said, 'As I die and in dying, live again, so you in dying will live also.' " "Insect, you are so slow. Let me take it," insisted Hare. Insect gave the message to Hare. Hare ran off fast and in his hurry, when he found man and woman, said, "Moon has sent you a message that in dying, Moon dies, so you too in dying shall perish." When Moon heard what Hare had said, Moon was angry and took a stick and hit Hare on the nose. That is why hares have split noses and men and women think that when they die, they perish.

This is Lent when we are aware of death. The most passionate sermon on death I ever read was written by a preacher two weeks after his 24-year-old son "beat his father to the grave." His message was one of rage. Not that death took his son, although that was certainly part of it, but because someone in his presence called it the "will of God." In great anguish and rage his faith exploded: "My own consolation lies in knowing that it was not the will of God that Alex die; that when the waves closed over the sinking car, God's heart was the first of all our hearts to break" (William Sloan Coffin).

Facing the prospect of a torturous, agonizing death on a cross, Jesus cried, "My heart is breaking. And what should I say, 'Father, save me from this hour'?"

49

Our text says that they came to Philip and said, "We wish to see Jesus," and Jesus answered, "The hour has come for the Son of Man to be glorified." And then he told them, "Unless a grain of wheat falls into the earth and dies, it remains just a single grain; but if it dies, it bears much fruit."

Living some three generations after the death and resurrection of Jesus, John wrote his "good news" to people who were risking their lives for Christ. To be a Christian meant facing one's immediate death, be it lion or cross. But Jesus had been there. Strength to face "a broken heart" can come from remembering Jesus too faced his own hour of heartbreak.

Whenever my deeply depressed grown son phones me to express the reality of his life, which is a broken one, and cries out in deep pain, my heart breaks anew. The cross of Christ invites us to participate in our own pain, to enter our emptiness, to discern our darkness.

"He was the sunshine of my day," moaned Kisa Gotami, as she rocked back and forth with her sorrow. Barely aware of her words, she changed them without thinking. "He *is* the sunshine of my day!" Kisa Gotami, called the Frail One, had nursed her son, the sunshine of her life, and as he grew, watched him play and run. Now, as she held her dead son in her lap, her sorrow was so great that she would not accept the boy's death. She took to the streets, carrying her dead son on her hip. Going from house to house, knocking at each door, she demanded, "Give me medicine for my son." The people saw that she was mad. They told her, "There is no medicine for the dead." But she acted as if she did not understand and only went on asking.

Now a certain wise old man saw Kisa Gotami and understood that it was her sorrow for her dead son that had driven her out of her mind. He did not mock her but said, "Go to the monastery. There is one there who might know of medicine for your son."

Seeing that the wise man spoke the truth, she went to the monastery and asked for medicine for her son. "This is what you must do. You must go to each house in the city, one by one, and from each you must seek tiny grains of mustard seed. But not just any house will do. You must only take mustard seeds from those houses in which no one has ever died."

Gotami agreed and began at once, knocking and saying, "I am Gotami. Please give me tiny grains of mustard seed for my son." When they brought her the seed, she added, "Before I take the seed, tell me, is this a house in which no one has died?" "Oh no, Gotami, the dead from this house are beyond counting." "Then I must go elsewhere."

She went from house to house, but always the answer was the same. In the entire city there was no house which death had not entered. Finally she understood why she had been sent on this hopeless task. She left the city, overcome with her feelings, and gave up her dead son. When she returned to the monastery, she said, "Most honored sir, there are no houses where death is not known. I see now that whoever is born must die. Everything passes away. There is no cure but the knowing."[1]

We hold death in common. Though science has pushed back its possibility in time, its inevitability surrounds us all. Everything dies ... fleas and flies, mice and men, all die. In order to make death less threatening, we personify it. We speak of death as an ugly hag, an old man, or even "the mother of beauty" (Wallace Stevens). Because we are aware of the proximity of death, we appreciate life's beauty here and now. We are hooked on living. Death is not only the mother of beauty but the equality. We are on a par with flies and fleas and flowers that die. But the Christian sees beyond death.

Yet it takes courage to die. A young boy dying of cancer gave Elisabeth Kubler-Ross a picture of a cannon with a large barrel aimed at a small boy with a stop sign in his hand, his interpretation of death, the great destroyer, before whom he felt helpless. Elisabeth accepted the picture and did not remove the cannon, as most of us would want to do, thus denying death. Instead, she drew a large figure next to the small one to assure him that he would not be alone. Three days later the boy gave her a picture of a peace bird on which was written, "This is my peace bird, and I have sunshine on my wings."

"Unless a seed dies ..." I once heard the story of a seven-year-old girl exploring the land of "Let's pretend" where it was dark, very, very dark, and cold, very, very cold; and she was lost, very lost. There was nothing she could do about it so she just lay down in the snow and died. This attitude permeated her every experience. She repudiated the idea that she could do anything about it and was constantly defeated by her own sense of inadequacy and her terror of life itself. Her intuition was correct. Her mother went away. There was a divorce, and the child was put in a boarding school. Forty years later the very sorrow of her loss worked its miracle, for what we experience is ours forever. She went into the darkness and found there a ray of hope that created a miracle of transformation, an insight into what life might be, and what she could do about it, and she said, "Yes," to life. Since death is part of life, she could say, "Yes," to death, as well, and meet it as a friend, opening a door into a new morning that she herself had made possible by her own deep change of attitude toward the force that works in every human heart, transforming the spirit. She who lives her life with compassion and creativity finds it.

As a youth Thor Heyerdahl, the famous sea adventurer, was afraid of water. He could not swim. Yet here he was, dipping the paddle of his canoe into the rapidly flowing river with his two friends. Suddenly he felt the canoe capsize and Thor was thrown into the water. When he surfaced, the canoe was racing toward the falls, and one of his companions was swimming toward the shore. With his fear of water and his heavy army clothes dragging him down, he knew that soon he would know which of his parents was right. His father believed in resurrection, the "Yes!" of life after death. His mother said, "No!" Thor's mind filled with the words of the Lord's Prayer and he prayed, and with the prayer burst the power of possibility. Each time he thought of giving up, a strange surge of strength came, and he went on. When his companion, clinging to the branch of a tree on the shore, stretched out his hand, Thor struggled toward it, and exhausted they drew the third one from the waters. That day Thor lost his fear of water and gained an insight into death — the assurance of his father's faith.

There is no cure for death. Death, as Gotami learned, is a part of life. There is a freedom that comes from accepting all of our fears, uncertainities, and sorrows, so well expressed in the prayer: God grant me the serenity to accept the things I cannot change, the courage to change the things I can, and the wisdom to know the difference. As Christians we add, "The cure is with God who creates life and creates new life, and the cosmic Christ of all creation, who said, 'The hour has come for the Son of Man to be glorified.' " In the cross of Christ we too glory. Amen and Amen.

Hymn of Response
"Lead On, O King Eternal" (words: Ernest W. Shurtleff, 1888; music: Henry Thomas Smart, c. 1835).

Prayers of the People, the Pastor, and The Lord's Prayer

Pastoral Prayer
Living Lord, help us become aware this Lenten season that preoccupation with our own sinfulness is preoccupation with ourself in history, ignoring our place in creation. Help us remember that unless a grain of wheat falls into the earth and dies, it remains just a single grain; but if it dies, it bears much fruit. Those who live life in compassion and creativity will find it.

Offering

Doxology

Hymn of Commitment
"Here I Am, Lord" (text and music, 1983, Daniel L. Schutte and New Dawn Music, P.O. Box 13248, Portland, Oregon 97215-0248).

Benediction
Go now in the name of God, who created the heaven and the earth and gives us much fruit, and in Jesus Christ, who showed us how to plant the seed and die the death, and the Holy Spirit, who gives fruition to the earth and to its creatures. Amen.

1. Adapted from Sheldon Kopp, *Metaphors from a Psychotherapist* (Palo Alta: Science and Behavior Book, 1971).

Palm Sunday

The Lord Has Need Of It

Call to Worship
"Say to them, 'The Lord needs it.'" Come, let us worship the Lord.
The Lord needs it!

Processional Hymn
"All Praise To Thee, For Thou, O King Divine (words: F. Bland
Tucker, 1938; music: Ralph Vaughn Williams, 1906).

Children's Time
*(Show pictures or flannel figures on a flannelboard of the itali-
cized words as you read the poem. Repeat the reading, inviting the
children to say the refrain with you: "It's Palm Sunday!" Young
children enjoy jumping up and standing as the refrain is spoken.)*

When leaves are budding on the *tree*,
And *birds* sing down their songs on me,
And *fish* swim upstream from the sea,
It's Palm Sunday!

When sunshine melts the *ice and snow*,
And blades of *grass* begin to grow,
And *lakes* and *rivers* overflow,
It's Palm Sunday!

When overhead the *skies* are blue,
And *sun* and *rain* bring life that's new,
And *calves* are born, and *kittens* too,
It's Palm Sunday!

When merry *crickets* squeal and sing,
It's time to thank God for the spring,
And for Palm Sunday! *(clap: Yeah!)*

Prayer of Confession
Dear Lord, we are foolish people with great needs who forget your need for our company, for being there for the little, the lost, and the least. Transform us from foolish people into "fools for Christ." In his name we pray. Amen.

Words of Assurance
God says to us as God said to Moses, "I will be with you." Amen.

Psalter Reading   Psalm 118:1-2, 19-29 or Psalm 31:9-16

Affirmation of Faith
I believe in God, who created a billion, billion stars, a planet blue and green, and a Savior rising from the grave, and in Jesus Christ who was that foolish, risen Savior, and the Holy Spirit who enables us to be "fools for Christ," filled with faith, and joy, and foolishness. Amen.

Old Testament   Isaiah 50:4-9a

Epistle Lesson   Philippians 2:5-11

New Testament   Mark 14:1-15—15:47

Sermon
This is a day for rejoicing.
This is the celebration of the king!
Let all the earth and heaven shout with joy.
The Lord needs it.
For he said, "Go into the village and bring me
The colt that has never been ridden."
Just say, "The Lord needs it."
A royal king?
One sent in the name of the Lord?
Occupant of an unbroken colt?
The Lord needs it?
This is the one to whom we shout, "Hosanna! Save us!"?
Discipleship can be difficult.

"Why are you untying the colt?" they asked.
"The Lord needs it."
Discipleship can make fools of us all.
For they threw their cloaks on the colt for Jesus to sit on.
And as he rode along, people kept spreading
Their cloaks on the way.
No need for masks nor sacred coverings this day.
This is the day for dancing.
This is the celebration of our Lord.
Blessed is the king who comes in the name of the Lord!
Peace in heaven and glory in the highest!
And suddenly there was a multitude
Praising God and saying,
"Glory to God in the highest heaven ..."
The stones of the earth,
The angels of the heaven,
The followers of Jesus
Praised God joyfully with a loud voice.
For this is the day for rejoicing!
This is the celebration of our Lord and King!
The Lord has need of it.

This is a joyful day, but in a world of sorrow and sadness, joyous people seem foolish. If we listen carefully to the story of Palm Sunday as written by Mark, it is a foolish story. The Lord needs a colt that has never been ridden? The disciples put their cloaks on the colt for Jesus to sit on? First, men wore two pieces of clothing, a cloak and their undergarments. Second, they set Jesus on all those cloaks on a small animal. What a foolish, fun-filled story! What a foolish people! Can you see Jesus wobbling back and forth on the back of a colt beside undressed disciples and others who spread their cloaks on the road? It is not often we associate foolishness with Jesus. Yet Paul did: "For the message about the cross is foolishness ... Has not God made foolish the wisdom of the world?" Our foolishness is in "Christ Jesus, who became for us wisdom and righteousness and sanctification and redemption, in order that, as it is written, 'Let the one who boasts, boast in the

Lord' " (1 Corinthians 1:10-31), and "If you think that you are wise in this age, you should become fools so that you may become wise" (1 Corinthians 3:10).

The most foolish people I know are children and poets. e e cummings was a "foolish" poet. He did not use captial letters to begin a sentence or a name. He wrote about a winter afternoon "at the magical hour when is becomes if" and a bespangled clown standing on eighth street handed him a flower. No one but cummings observed the clown because he was a mystery most people fear most; "he was alive, completely alert and miraculously whole; mind, heart, soul, a fine not a coarse clown, not saying a word, who was anything but dumb; since the silence in himself sang like a bird ... I thank heaven somebody's crazy."

A class of clowns in the midst of a serious academic day, on a serious academic campus, were giving away money, food, fruit, and candy. When these ran out, they exchanged silent blessings by placing their hands on the heads of people they met. When the vice president for development was told, "The clowns are here, but they're not talking," he replied, "Not with words, they're not."[1]

Jesus spoke not with words of the good news of the gospel. To believe that good news, which is too good to be true, is to become a fool for God. Yet, when we see everything dressed in paradox, clothed in contradiction, and learn that tension is energy that leads to creativity, we wonder whether we could be otherwise.

God's fool is one who enters the marketplace, the hospital, the school, for God's sake, for the role of the fool is that of the suffering servant. To be a fool for God is to celebrate life, to celebrate the little and the least whom Jesus loved, and to celebrate a new world, new and whole, different from the world in which we live. Jesus leads that parade!

From the beginning of Jesus' ministry there was fear of foolishness. The people said of the Nazarene carpenter who preached that the kingdom of God was at hand, "He is beside himself." What a foolish man!

Later, the disciples dismissed the good news of the women who ran from the tomb, saying, "He is risen!" They called their news an "idle tale" told by foolish women!

58

Even later, Christ's most persistent preacher, Paul, preached the cross "a stumbling block to Jews and foolishness to Gentiles." I know people who think in their hearts, "What fools these Christians be!" Yet it is from this foolish good news we receive our hope, for what divine madness to create "a billion, billion stars, a planet blue and green, and a Savior rising from the grave."[2]

Nasrudin was a famous Sufi foolish wiseman. He once lost his donkey and became frantic. At last he offered a reward to whomever would find his beast. The reward was the donkey! "Nasrudin! Nasrudin!" exclaimed the people. "How foolish you are. You are giving away what you are looking for!" Nasrudin smiled. "There are two blessings in this life. One is to find what you love. The other is to give it away."

The people cheered a foolish man on the way to the cross. He had found the life he was to give away. That is the foolishness we celebrate today.

It is in the imagination that we are set free from limitations on the possible. Yet how often we suspect joy and imagination. The psalmists used their power of joy and imagination in praise of God, singing, "Let the floods clap their hands" (Psalm 98:8). And the Christian poet Christopher Smart wrote a poem, "Rejoice in the Lamb," in which one of the lines reads: "The Great Flabber Dabber Flat Clapping Fish with Hands." The church lacked the imagination and joy of the poet and the psalmist and locked the former in an asylum because he would fall on his knees and pray on the street corners, imploring the people to pray with him. Foolish man! His contemporaries could not understand and thought he was a fool, believing he was mad. Later scholarship showed that he was not so crazy after all. At the end of his flabber dabber line, he wrote a note telling people to look up *Anson's Voyage* and Psalm 98. *Anson's Voyage* was a popular work of natural history and one of its illustrations showed flat fish jumping out of the water and seals with fins as hands.

Christopher Smart was a foolish man. So was Mark Twain who admitted such, "Ah, well, I am a great and sublime fool ... but then I am God's fool, and all His works must be contemplated with respect."

On Palm Sunday a foolish people followed a foolish messiah. From where does our "wise foolishness" come today? It comes from the wild and wonderful preachers and teachers, poets and spiritual guides. To live in their world of joy, imagination, and sacred story is to sense the Spirit and have the power of the mind over the possibility of things. Wonder is the parent of that possibility and her sibling is imagination. Faith is rooted in wonder and watered with imagination. Our perception of life is formed and fed and transformed by our faith imagination.

We are fools for the sake of Christ, taught by the Spirit, so that we may become wise, not in the wisdom of this world but boasting and rejoicing in the Lord. Come, join the parade. Hosanna in the highest! In the name of the Father, the Son, and the Holy Spirit. Amen.

Hymn of Response
"Rejoice, Ye Pure In Heart" (words: Edward H. Plumptre,1865; music: Arthur H. Messiter, 1889).

Prayers of the People, the Pastor, and The Lord's Prayer

Pastoral Prayer
Dear Lord, we worship you out of our need to express our thanksgiving for life and love and laughter. We know you have no need for this worship and yet we wonder if we were created out of your need for our love, for we are a foolish people before your mystery and majesty.

Palm Sunday is our reminder of Jesus' joyfulness in creation, in fellowship with people, and in parades and celebrations.

Renew in us a vision of your foolishness in its fullness, where floods clap their hands, morning stars sing together, and all the heavenly beings shout for joy. Thy kingdom come. Thy will be done. Amen.

Offering

Doxology

Hymn of Commitment

"Jesus Calls Us" (words: Cecil Frances Alexander, 1852; music: William H. Jude, 1874).

Benediction

Go now in the name of God who is with us, and Jesus Christ who is sent, and the Holy Spirit who sends us into the world with God's good news, "I am with you always, even unto the end of the world." Amen.

---

1. Maria Harris, *Teaching and the Religious Imagination* (San Francisco, California: Harper & Row, 1987).

2. Thomas H. Troeger, *Imagining a Sermon* (Nashville, Tennessee: Abingdon Press, 1998).

Jesus, The Servant

Call to Worship
"Jesus, the Master, rose from the table, took off his robe and washed his disciples' feet." Come, let us worship the Servant of God.

Processional Hymn
"For The Beauty Of The Earth" (words: Folliot S. Pierpoint, 1864; music: Conrad Kocher, 1838; arr. by W. H. Monk, 1861).

Children's Time
In our sacred story for today we read how Jesus was the Servant of God. He washed the feet of his disciples. A small girl, her arms full of books, walked through the park, thinking, as she looked at an old man, "It must be strange to be old and sit in the cold on a small park bench in a great coat." Just then the old man lifted his head and saw the girl watching him and he asked, "Yes?" "I just thought," the girl stammered. "I wondered ... do you need ... you look ... might I ... can I help you?" The old man smiled as he said, "You already have."

Talk About
How did the girl help the old man? What are some of the ways we can show love and be a "servant" for God?

Prayer of Confession
Dear Lord, forgive all of the times we have neglected the stranger or even those in our homes. Fill our hearts and minds with compassion, care for others and for creation. Forgive our selfishness in thinking of and caring only for ourselves. In the name of Christ, Servant of God. Amen.

Words of Assurance
God said, "I have loved you with an everlasting love" (Jeremiah 31:3).

Psalter Reading   Psalm 116:1-4, 12-19

Old Testament   Exodus 12:1-4 (5-10) 11-14

Epistle Lesson   1 Corinthians 11:23-26

New Testament   John 13:1-17, 31b-35

Sermon
When a brother visited the hermits in the desert and saw them working, he asked, "Why do you work for the bread that perishes? Mary has chosen the best part, to sit at the feet of the Lord without working." The Abbot told his disciple to give the brother a book and a cell and there he left him all day to read. At the ninth hour he looked out to see if the Abbot was going to call him to dinner and at last set out to find him. "Did the brethren not eat today, Father?" "Oh, yes, we have just eaten," the Abbot replied. "Why did you not call me?" he asked. "You are a spiritual man and do not need this food that perishes," the Abbot said. "Forgive me, Father," said the brother. The Abbot replied, "It was because Martha worked that Mary was able to learn."[1]

Jesus and his friends were eating together. Before we eat we wash our hands. In Jesus' time it was the feet. Feet that had walked in sandals through the garbage and debris of market street filled with smelly fish heads and bones, rotten, putrid fruit, and donkey droppings were stretched out across the floor, as the disciples reclined before the low table, eating together. Jesus, the honored one, the Master, arose from the table, took off his robe, and washed his disciples' feet.

Jesus knew that the meaning of life was the good news of God's love and our response of love and service. He taught "Love one another as I have loved you," and showed us how.

64

We long for such love. In Tennessee Williams' play, *A Streetcar Named Desire*, Blanche longed desperately to be loved. She was not easy to love, however, because she talked too much and the way she talked repelled those from whom she wished love. When Blanche met Mitch, overweight, lonely, and in need of love, as well, she shared with him one of the tragic moments in her life and Mitch took her in his arms. "You need somebody. I need somebody. Could it be you and me, Blanche?" Blanche stared at Mitch, her eyes filled with tears, as she reached out for him, saying, "Sometimes there's God, so quickly," and the scene closed.

To say to anyone, "I love you," is tantamount to saying, "You shall live forever." Only authentic love is expansive, humble, and generous, for in the presence of love there are miracles. Happiness depends on love. But to become love in human form, to become servant, is a reversal of our culture's values. Love is different from what our culture teaches. It is to value others as they are, rather than what we want them to be, and to desire the others' needs be met in order for them to live abundantly.

Jesus said for us to love our neighbor as ourself, therefore, love yourself, and we love because God loves us. One of the things I love and enjoy is reading essays, "talking with" the writer (dead or alive). As I sat with Loren Eisely in the dark, he told me about his insomnia, and my hankering for friendship was satisfied. His conversation was eloquent. I can hear him now, polishing every phrase until it shone, and I wondered how often we take advantage of diving beneath the surface of polite talk: "How are you? How are the children? What do you think about the election? Do you think it will snow?"

Here I was sitting with a great anthropologist while he told me the secrets of his night. Nor did I have to be rude and ask him to stop while I gathered together my own thoughts and feelings on the matter. Closing the book, it was my turn to speak, and imagine, a marvelously imaginative, brillant writer fell silent, listening!

Of course we can so engage all print, but essays, because they are short, honest, and relevant, are honed to a fine edge. They are the refined jewels of reflection, and we share that beauty with others.

To enter Eiseley's bedroom and endure his sleepless night is to sit beside his bed in his lonely room, as he tosses in his dreams, knitting the universe together with his dark thoughts. Then, hearing the earth shake from the drum roll of the surf, he rises to dress and saunter forth, summoning from the white spray the features and faces of the dead he knows. This sufferer of insomnia, this talker who cannot sleep, has shattered mine. I rise to leave but he stops me with his musing.

"Beareth all things, believeth all things, hopeth all things, endureth all things." Paul's words on the lips of the insomniac soothed my spirit. I feel in safe territory and sit again to listen to his final soliloquy: Stranded in an empty airport in the middle of the night in a strange city in a foreign country, dead tired, having missed his plane for which he must now wait until morning, longing to be home, he saw approach him an amazing conglomeration of sticks and broken, misshapen pulleys which made up the body of a man. His mind rang out with despair, as he thought Paul's words: "Wretched man that I am, who will save me?" And then his own: How could we for a single moment imagine that thought or wonder or wisdom would save us? His words mesmerized me as that figure entered Eiseley, contorting his shape, transforming his doubt into hope, again with Paul's words: "Beareth all things, believeth...." Believe, believe. This is the thread that weaves the night's dying into tomorrow's birth. "I, who do not sleep, can tell you this," he whispered. And then the immortal words: "And now faith, hope, and love abide, these three; and the greatest of these is love."

Failure to love is to live a lie, to be out of harmony with our true self, pursuing the wrong goals for the wrong reasons and caring more about other people's opinions than serving God. Jesus washed the feet of his disciples out of the harmony of his true self.

Out of that harmony we serve: raising and teaching children, cooking meals, tending flower or vegetable gardens, recycling cans and paper, saving water and energy, being there for the other, participating in rituals of worship and celebration, taking care of our mother earth, and gathering the offerings of the community in time, money, talent.

Jesus as God's servant knew the meaning of love and said, "Come unto me, all you who labor, and I will give you rest." A well-known sculptor had a burning ambition to create the greatest statue of Jesus Christ ever made. He began in his oceanside studio by shaping a clay model of a triumphant, regal figure. The head was thrown back and the arms were upraised in a gesture of great majesty. It was his conception of how Christ would look: strong and victorious. "This will be my masterpiece," he said, on the day the clay model was completed. During the night, however, a heavy fog rolled into the area and sea spray seeped through a partially opened window. The moisture affected the shape of the clay so that when the artist returned to the studio in the morning, he was shocked at what he found. Drops of moisture had formed on the model an illusion of bleeding or weeping. The head had drooped. The facial expression had been transformed into one of compassion. And the arms had dropped into a posture of welcome. It had become a wounded Christ-figure. The artist stared at the figure, agonizing over the time wasted and the need to begin all over again. Then, meaning came to him. He began to see that this image of Christ was, by far, the truer one. So he carved these words in the base of the newly shaped figure: "Come Unto Me."

Whether we sit at Jesus' feet to learn as Mary did or serve at Jesus' feet as Martha did, may we follow in the footsteps of our Lord, the Servant of God, in the name of the Parent, the Son, and the Holy Spirit. Amen.

Eucharist Hymn
"Bread Of The World" (words: Reginald Heber, 1827; John S. B. Hodges, 1868).

The Celebration of the Eucharist

Prayers of the People, the Pastor, and The Lord's Prayer

Pastoral Prayer
(A Psalm of Creation)
Let the lambs bleat,
    the goats leap,
    the mountains clap their hands for joy.
    The earth is the Lord's and everything in it.

When the morning stars sing together,
    let the cattle moo,
    the doves coo,
    the waters pour forth their praise.
    The earth is the Lord's and everything in it.

You fill the hills with flocks and flowers,
    the valleys with fields of grain
    the deer drink from your pools of pleasure,
    the dolphins dance in your deep,
    the falcon flies,
    the earth lies full with your abundance.
    The earth is the Lord's and everything in it.

You are my sun by day
    my moon by night,
    as welcome as rain in a dry and thirsty desert.

In you I trust,
    the earth is yours,
    blessed be God, our Creator.

Offering

Doxology

Hymn of Dismissal
"Lord, Dismiss Us With Thy Blessing" (words: attr. to John Fawcett, 1773; music: *The European Magazine and Review*, 1792).

Benediction

Go now into the world in the name of God, who creates and serves out of love, and Jesus Christ, the Servant of God, and the Holy Spirit, who inspires and enables us to love. In Christ's name. Amen.

---

1. Thomas Merton, *The Wisdom of the Desert* (New York: New Directions, 1960).

Good Friday

Crumbs From The Cross

Call to Worship
Jesus said, "It is finished." Come, let us worship God who completes creation and redemption.

Processional Hymn
"Lift High The Cross" (words: George William Kitchin and Michael Robert Newbolt, 1916; music: Sydney Hugo Nicholson, 1916).

Children's Time
There is an old make-believe story about the man in the moon looking down on earth and seeing a rabbit, a monkey, and a fox warming themselves around a fire and sharing their supper together, for they were good friends. The moon said to the stars, "I am going to take a trip to earth," and the moon said good-bye to the stars. With all the time he had to think through the eons and eons of time, and being curious, with much imagination, he often wondered which of the three, the rabbit, the monkey, or the fox, was the kindest?

Wanting to know but not wanting them to know him, he changed himself into an old and poor beggar. "Please help me," cried the beggar, as he approached the three friends. "I am sooo hungry." "How sad," said the three friends, hurrying off to find food for the poor man.

The monkey quickly found some bananas in a tree, the fox caught a fish in the brook nearby, but the rabbit could not find any food for the poor man. Tears filled the rabbit's eyes, but he knew that feeling sorry would not feed the hungry man, so he used his imagination and his thinking and soon he had an idea and a plan.

"Mr. Monkey, would you gather some firewood for me," said the rabbit, "and Mr. Fox would you make me a fire with the wood?" They did as the rabbit asked and soon the fire burned brightly. Then the rabbit said to the beggar, "I do not have any food to share with you, but I will give you all that I have. When I am cooked, you may eat me."

The rabbit was about to jump into the fire, when the beggar, the man in the moon, cried, "No! You are very kind, but do not harm yourself." The three friends were amazed as the poor man changed into the man-in-the-moon. "You are the kindest animal I have ever met," he said to the rabbit. "I will take you up into the sky to live with me."

So he did and that is why some nights when you look up at the moon and it is shining brightly, you can see the rabbit, the kindest of them all, for he was the one willing to give his own life to help another live.

Prayer of Confession

Dear Lord, we, like Peter, disappoint you, but may we, like Peter, "be there" with you. Forgive us when we run away and desert you. Give us courage for the living of this day, lifting high the cross to remember your courage. Amen.

Words of Assurance

"Lo, I am with you always, even unto the end of the world."

Psalter Reading   Psalm 22

Old Testament   Isaiah 52:13—53:12

Epistle Lesson   Hebrews 10:16-25

New Testament   John 18:1—19:42

Sermon

They are eating our hope tonight,
Tearing at the Bread
Hanging limp upon the tree,
Who once was sung to tenderly
In a manger on a silent night.

This "Good" Friday the heavens are angry,
Shouting curses at a sleeping world
That in the morning will awake
To a famine of faith.
Feed us this day, O Lord,
From crumbs fallen from the cross,
We who are oblivious of the Feast to come.
God, give us faith enough to face the dragon
That devours our vow to love,
Or with our lack of courage, hold our hand
Until the dragon shrinks.

Good Friday reminds us of our fear. As a child I loathed Good Friday! My mother and I groped our way down the dark church aisle, the windows having been covered with thick black cloths. The organ groaned the first hymn, echoing the atmosphere. The funereal voices of the ministers sounded as hounds wailing at the moon, on and on and on ... From noon until three there would be six sections of thirty minutes each, six somber black-robed ministers preaching, one after another, as we sang them sadly into their place.

I squirmed on the hard pew and took a quick unsuspected, sidelong glance at my mother's passive face. Was she really interested? This was certainly the dullest place I could imagine, for I had been taught well by preachers in horn-rimmed glasses on small, peaked noses, under squinty eyes, shouting, "Imagination is the work of the devil! Keep your mind on Scripture at all times!" On Good Friday I wondered who suffered more, Jesus on the cross, or me in the church? And immediately I prayed for fogiveness. But at last it was time for communion and I quickly stood up and headed for the aisle, for this meant "The End"! I was no sooner up than my mother grabbed my hand to keep me safely in harbor. At snail pace we crept to the altar. There I kneeled before the black draped cross as the minister held the cup before me. As he tipped the cup, I lifted my head and the dark red liquid ran down my dress. He moved on to the next person, unaware of the wounded victim he had left behind.

How many wounded victims does Good Friday leave behind?

"Crucify him!" the ugly, angry mob shouts, the crown of thorns digging deeper into his temple, his head bleeding, his hands bound, his body beaten. The words of denial by his friend, "I know not the man," rang in his ears, as he dragged the heavy cross among the mocking and jeering of the cruel crowd. Then he felt the nails tear into his flesh and the tormenting thirst, the piercing doubt.

A parishioner said to the pastor as he hung Emil Nolde's picture of the burial of Jesus, a yellow, pain-shriveled body, *The Entombment*, "I wish you'd take that picture down. It's awful. It makes Jesus look so dead." She proceeded to tell him which Pieta to hang in its place, adding, "It shows Jesus as smooth-skinned and athletic."

"Crucified, dead, and buried." The ancient words filed into the minister's mind and marched through his head as a procession of monks.[1]

Good Friday reminds us that death is awful. I have encountered death's awfulness in two fathers. The first was snatched quickly by a swiftly moving train, the second slowly by a debilitating, devouring cancer. Death is awful. "Put something else in its place, please." I would rather hide my head in the sand than face the pain of identification with that death, and yet because of that death I can say, "I know God understands our pain because Jesus suffered pain upon the cross." Jesus was fully human. He hurt. He cried. He ate and drank. He experienced the awfulness of death as he hung on a cross. And yet sometimes I think we know the story so well we pass it by. Only when we experience it do we open the ears of our heart.

Jesus' death on the cross was a voluntary act whereby the symbol of the cross as torturous death was transformed into unconditional love. Old things must pass away before the new can come. When we do not see Jesus' death as death, because we see it through eyes acquainted with resurrection, and therefore both are diminished, our souls are not drowned in delight, because we have not first despaired. We had been told the story, but we have not experienced it.

74

Dante's pilgrimage took him through the Otherworld, from a hell to a purgatory to a paradise. He tells the story of his journey of the spirit into the realm that lies beyond death. "In the middle of the course of life, I found myself in a dark wood." Dante looked for and found God in the depth and heigth of human experience. As he voyaged into the unknown, he discovered a life beyond fear, beyond death, in the assurance of the love that moves the sun and the other stars.

It was over. A life that had begun with so much promise snuffed out in a second of time. One minute he was laughing and talking and enjoying life, and the next the sudden "bang" of a blowout, the curb, the tree, a life blown out, and it was over. When she first heard the news, she felt numb. It was not true. It could not happen! She saw his grin, as he left earlier that evening, saying, "I'll see ya!" His years flashed before her eyes and her numbness turned to tears. She sobbed softly, for there would be no more Christmases, nor Easters, nor birthdays, no more, "Thanks, Mom!" Her sobs grew into screams of anger. "Why?" she shouted.

She was alone. To whom was she shouting? If God was there, if God was the source of her life, then God must understand her confusion and her pain. Exhausted at last, she asked for strength, for there seemed to be no answers.

Her son was more than a body. He was part of her being. Now there would be no more anxiety over his frustrated hopes and dreams, no more nightly vigils during his illnesses, no more unanswered questions for him. If God was Lord of life, Architect of creation, death too was part of God's plan, and if God could create life out of nothing, God could continue life after death, she thought.

"In the beginning, God," she sighed and slowly rose, as if leaving her cross. The pain would always be there, but perhaps time would allow her to live again for those who needed her love. She had only her trust in God's promise and her knowledge that God too had lost a son to death. Perhaps there would be another Easter victory!

"Where is God?" we ask in our pain, our sorrow, our fear.

"Where is God?" the people asked.

Here God is — hanging on a cross.

Here is God — collecting our tears.

Here God is — with us now.

Good Friday asks us to examine our fear in relationship to God, to let go of our mooring posts of security and swim in the ocean of life with all its doubts, disappointments, and death, to discover the healing, reconciling Spirit within, the meaning of our faith, the message of Good Friday. Amen.

Hymn of Response
"What Wondrous Love Is This" (words: USA folk hymn; harm. Paul J. Christiansen, 1955).

Prayers of the People, the Pastor, and The Lord's Prayer

Pastoral Prayer
Living God, this is a dark day, and yet we know that the growth of the human person takes place in the dark. In that darkness we learn to trust the empty spaces and the silences. This is a day of pain, which leads to compassion, and identification with others, our brothers and sisters in suffering. Receive our prayers and our praise, you who are our all in all. Amen.

Offering

Doxology

Hymn of Commitment
"Beneath The Cross Of Jesus" (words: Elizabeth C. Clephane, 1872; music: Frederick C. Maker, 1881).

Benediction
Go now into the world in the name of God who heals and redeems, transforming the cruelty of the cross into the power of God's love, and Jesus Christ who leads us into, through, and out of our pain and suffering, and the Holy Spirit who prays for us. Amen.

---

1. Thomas H. Troeger, *Creating Fresh Images for Preaching* (Valley Forge: Judson Press, 1982).

Standing On The Shore

Call to Worship
"I am the resurrection and the life" (John 11:25). Come, let us worship the Lord of life together.

Processional Hymn
"Christ The Lord Is Risen Today" (words: Charles Wesley, 1739; music: Lyra Davidica, 1708).

Children's Time
"He is dead! It is over. Our hope is destroyed." Jesus' friends sat in the dark room, remembering his words and his works, especially his last day, that sad Friday. "It felt as if the world were angry," said one of his friends. "Yes, I can still hear the thunder growling in the sky and the lightning ripping open the earth. I was afraid," admitted another. "Will it ever be light again?" The others shook their heads. "No, the sun will never shine for us again. The light of our world has gone out."

Those gathered cried, for they missed their friend. They cried because what they had hoped would now never happen. The long night was dark with pain, especially the pain of their denial. "We should have died with him. Why did we flee and not fight for our Master?" The dark night of despair grew longer, but the next day was worse. The sun still did not shine. The world was silent and still. They fell on their knees and prayed. The day flowed into the even darker night and they prayed on.

Deep in prayer they did not hear her come, as she threw open the door and sunlight flooded the room. "The sun is dancing!" Mary cried. "The world is alive again!" Blinking in the bright sunlight, they ran to the window. Some of them rushed outside to see for themselves. The sun was indeed dancing! "The sun is shining. It is a new day!" they cried to one another. Mary shouted, "Jesus is risen!" "Christ is risen!" they all shouted with joy, and the sun-filled world seemed to reply, "He is risen indeed!"

Prayer of Confession

Eternal Parent, we are afraid of death and all that diminishes life. We seek answers to the mystery of this threatening agent that snuffs out our breathing and leaves those of us who remain feeling helpless and lonely. Forgive our doubts as we hear the holy story of resurrection. Forgive our greed as if there were no tomorrow, as if you had not conquered the powers of death. Fill our lives with faith. In Christ's name. Amen.

Words of Assurance

"Thou wilt not leave us in the dust
Thou madest man, he knows not why;
He thinks he was not made to die;
And thou hast made him: thou art just"
(Tennyson, "In Memoriam," Prologue, st. iii).

Psalter Reading   Psalm 118:1-2, 14-24

Epistle Lesson   1 Corinthians 15:1-11

New Testament   John 20:1-18 or Mark 16:1-8

Sermon

His presence began early this morning in the dawn,
when the birds sing and sight is dim,
whispering to us, "Why is the stone rolled away?"
"Where is his body?"
"Who is this light dressed in a white robe seated on the right?"
How did they hear, "He is not here. He has risen as he told you."
Trembling before such mystery,
Fearing, they fled.

Paul wrote, "Lo! I tell you a mystery ... the perishable does not inherit the imperishable, the body is raised a spiritual body," whatever that means. Oh, the mystery and the wonder of it!

The witnesses to the mystery did not shout, "Hallelujah!" as we did this morning. They did not sing with tremenduous joy, "Christ the Lord is risen today," as we did. Instead, trembling, they fled. They were terrified. In their fear, they fled from the tomb.

They had come in despair, their dreams dashed, but such is disillusionment. Finally, we accept it. But to witness a miracle, believe what is impossible is possible, always confronted with the surprises of God, too much mystery is too much. Trembling, we flee. Better to let the dream die, bury it, than face God's actions in the mystery of death.

We experience the words of the poet:

All that we do
Is touched with ocean, yet we remain
On the shore of what we know.[1]

We remain on the shore of what we know. On Easter we come to the empty tomb looking for answers, but mystery is not a matter of the mind but astonishment and awe, seeing from the soul.

"And they went out and fled from the tomb, for trembling and astonishment had come upon them...."

"This is not Thou, O Lord. Yet Thou art in this also." Mystery encourages us to be modest before radical amazement. "We speak the wisdom of God in a mystery" (1 Corinthians 2:7). There is Something More beyond belief, beyond "the door."

Yet we remain on the shore of what we know.

When imagination fails we cannot walk on water nor stop the storm. We stand and stare at the sea on the shore of what we know. Only Jesus did. He stopped the storm and the sea lay down. Is it possible that with enough awe and wonder at mystery and with enough passion over possibility we might perhaps do so?

"All that we do is touched with ocean" and possibility. That is the mystery and the miracle of Easter. The seeker approached the disciple and asked respectfully, "What is the meaning of human life?" The disciple consulted the works of his master and confidently replied, "Human life is nothing but the expression of God's

79

exuberance." When the seeker addressed the master himself with the same question, the master said, "I do not know."

We never know. We only leap to accept the best life has to offer, for Easter is a gift of love and perfect love casts out fear.

The text says that they "said nothing to anyone, for they were afraid." The questions remain, the seeking for answers continues, but though the questions remain unanswered, accepting the gift of Easter, of Christ's resurrection, feels like one.

Once I was closely involved with a dying friend. We daily visited her in her own home, surrounded by her family and friends. She had not been shuffled off to a hospital where she would have "better care." She remained at home where she had the best possible care, administered with love and dignity, and there death became a welcome Guest rather than a feared Enemy. Death is a transition, another stage in the process of life whose extent and duration are beyond our knowledge. In the presence of God's love death loses its power. The future becomes open.

"In my Father's house are many rooms; if it were not so, I would have told you. I am going there to prepare a place for you." Easter is God calling, "Enter!" Easter is Christ's invitation to his Parent's House. Easter is the symbol of what can happen to us, about the experience of being made new, when we do not have the power to do so. It is not dogmas and doctrines that comfort us in crises. It is Jesus who comes to comfort us, for through the story and his words we are given — Christ!

The promise of the gospel is God's victory over death and the mission of the church is to bring life where there is death, freedom where there is oppression, love where there is hate, compassion where there is apathy, and hope where there is despair.

Do you remember the movie *Dead Poets' Society*? In it the English teacher in a private boys' school attempted to open their hearts and eyes to feel and think and experience for themselves. He lost his job because of it, but the film closed in triumph. The boys, in recognition of their appreciation for the teacher's efforts, "rose up" to stand on their desks, as he had shown them his way of seeing things from a different point of view. Resurrection is the story of how Jesus "rose up" to help us see from his point of view.

Pastor Merrill could not be comforted enough by reading only Isaiah but also Lamentations at the funeral of Owen Meany. The fingers of his pale hand moved in and out of the shaft of sunlight, like minnows. Then to Psalms and on into the New Testament, that little bit of bravery from Romans. Then First Corinthians and Second and the Twenty-third Psalm. And when everyone was seated, he said, "O God, how we miss Owen Meany!" Then he read to them that passage about the miracle in the Gospel according to Mark, "O God, give us back Owen Meany!"

With Pastor Merrill and John, Owen Meany's best friend and the narrator of the novel, we cry, "Give us back Christ!"[2]

The story is unended for the story goes on. Each of us writes an ending by the way we live and move and have our being, for we are God's stories, and through prayer and the sacred story we can love, hear our name called, and believe, for "these stories were written so that you may believe that Jesus is the Christ, the son of God, and by believing have life in his name." Christ is risen!

Hymn of Response
"Easter People, Raise Your Voices" (words: William M. James, 1979; music: Henry T. Smart, 1867).

Prayers of the People, the Pastor, and The Lord's Prayer

Pastoral Prayer
Dear God, like frolicking waves we jostle among the crowd on Palm Sunday. Like angry waves we cry for his crucifixion on Wild Wednesday. Like fearful disciples we seek our safety and plead for God's power on Maundy Thursday. "Forgive them," he said on Good Friday. And on the third day he arose *and the sea lay down.* Amen.

Affirmation of Faith
I know that my redeemer lives to bless me with his love.
He lives to grant me daily breath here on earth and heaven above.
Christ is risen. He is risen indeed!

Offering

Doxology

Hymn of Commitment
"Thine Is the Glory" (words: Cantate Domino, World Student Christian Federation; music: George Frederick Handel).

Benediction
Go now in the name of God who gives us resurrection and new life, and Jesus the Christ who shows us what the resurrection and life can mean, and the Holy Spirit who enables us to live that resurrection now. Amen.

----

1. Richard Wilbur, "For Dudley," *New and Collected Poems* (New York: Harcourt Brace Jovanovich, 1988), p. 135.

2. John Irving, *A Prayer For Owen Meany* (New York: Ballantine, 1989).

Lenten Poetry

Did You Know?

Did you know
Dust creates the snow?
Common, useless, nuisance dust
Creates the soft, delicious stuff
Of white and lovely, lacy snow?
Did you know?

Did you know
That pain can be
Author of strength and beauty, accompanying
The hurt that causes life to grow?
Did you know?

Did you know
That God once did
The unbelievable and hid
Within a gruesome, horrible death
Upon a cross, the breath
Of life and love, forgiving foe
And friend alike.
Did you know?
Oh, did you know?

Maundy Thursday

A guarded look,
    a crooked finger,
        the smirch spreading,
            the tongue twisting its tail,
            and then the kiss —

Hell opened its jaws and he walked within
    without a sword or shield or angel voices.

Betrayed,
    he held his injury in his arms,
    as a mother holds an angry child,
    rocking it into sleep.

So when it woke
    it rose and smiled —
        a glorious wound.

Resurrection: The Living Word

Dead, rotted words lay limp upon the cold, tomb-slab,
    wrapped in death's white linen cloths,
    which once had hung upon the cross,
    hope leaking out and with it life.

Fat dogma, pompous law had nailed them there,
    a warning to the rest:
    "Imagination is a leper. Do not touch."

Authorities have power, as parent-tapes
    of "Do's," and "Don't's" and "Can't's" and "Should's,"
    and fear the raging spirit in their midst,
    so kill the words and wrap them in
    white linen sheets within a tomb
    or bind them in a sacred book.

Yet early on that morning when she came
    to seek the spirit of the living word,
    all that she saw were linen shrouds,
    not tossed aside nor torn to shreds,
    but chaos conquered, folded carefully.

For on that Sunday with the sun they rose,
    shook off decay,
    grave's grey garments,
    rolled the stone away,
    to challenge, comfort and console,
    and once again incarnate
    the presence of God's living word.

The World Cup

They were playing their hearts out before our very eyes.
They were playing "for keeps."
But the Cup could not be kept.

Were they playing then for pleasure, for the fun of it?
No, their passion to win poured out of the screen.
They were playing, as I said, their hearts out.
I know. I saw some of them bleeding on the stadium floor.

It reminded me of churches playing their hearts out
To win Christ to keep on their mantel
To display to each other their championship,
While his heart bleeds on the world's floor.

Little Lamb

Little lamb,
Meek and mild,
Symbol of the Advent Child,
Were you there that day?
Did you at his manger bleat?
Did you kneel there at his feet,
Where he lay upon the hay?

Little lamb,
Did you know
He, like you,
One day would grow
To be sacrificed?
Little lamb, did you know
That small Child would be ...
The Christ?
Did you know?